LESSONS
TO MY
YOUNGER SELF

Navigating Through Workplace Discrimination, Racism, and Sexism

FAYE IRVING

ISBN 979-8-89130-679-0 (paperback)
ISBN 979-8-89130-680-6 (digital)

Christian Faith Publishing
832 Park Avenue
Meadville, PA 16335
www.christianfaithpublishing.com

All biblical citations were taken from the New International Version of the Holy Bible unless otherwise indicated.

Printed in the United States of America

To my precious daughter, Amber.

To my nieces and other young women
navigating the early journey of life.

CONTENTS

BEING BLACK IN THE WORKPLACE

They take my kindness for weakness.
They take my silence for speechless.
They consider my uniqueness strange.
They call my language slang.
They see my confidence as conceit.
They see my mistakes as defeat.
They consider my success accidental.
They minimize my intelligence to "potential."
My questions mean "I'm unaware."
My advancement is somehow unfair.
Any praise is preferential treatment.
To voice concern is discontentment.
If I stand up for myself, I'm too defensive.
If I don't trust them, I'm too apprehensive.
I'm defiant! If I separate.
I'm fake if I assimilate.
Yet, constantly I am faced with work place hate.
My character is constantly under attack.
Pride for my race makes me, "TOO BLACK."
(Linda Sharp)

Yet, I can only be me. And, who am I you ask? I am that Strong Black Person… Who stands on the back of my ancestor's achievements, with an erect spine pointing to the stars with pride, dignity and respect which lets the work place in America know, that I not only possess the ability to play by the rules, but I can make them as well!
(Black History 365)

CHAPTER 1

Happy Twenty-Fifth Birthday, Amber

This book is dedicated to my dearest daughter, Amber, and a host of my nieces, whom I love and cherish. My desire is also for other young ladies entering the independence phase of their lives to benefit from my experience and recommendations.

Early in life, you are told what to do, how to do it, when it should be done, and why. You are now moving from the comfort of a childhood at home into a world where you are the decision-maker, and you will soon run your own home. Transitioning into adulthood can feel overwhelming because suddenly you are expected to make all the decisions and have all the answers. Life will come at you from so many angles, and some will not be desirable. You must be grounded in a foundation beyond your will, knowledge, and wit. Otherwise, it is simply not enough to "manage" this journey called life.

As a young African American woman, you will soon discover the world is not fair. It is well documented that the deck is stacked against you being female, young, and Black. While that does not mean you are destined for failure, it *does* mean you need an anchor to support your existence. While this book has biblical references, it is not about religion. It is about a relationship with a power that is beyond our comprehension and is present all around us, willing to lead, guide, and protect. My foundation is in God, and that is the premise for the recommendations presented here as your guidance along life's journey.

Allow me to share some highlights from McKinsey & Company, which paired up with Lean In to dig deeper into the reality and disparities of women in the workplace.

McKinsey & Company is the oldest and largest of the "Big Three" management consultancies and the world's most prestigious strategy consulting firm.

Lean In has a mission to document the realities of working women and provide strategies to mitigate the disparities: "We help women achieve their ambitions and work to create an equal world."

These reputable groups teamed together to produce the research study *Women in the Workplace*, which is the largest study on the state of women in corporate America. The highlights I will reference are cited from the 2022 study, which details information collected from 333 participating organizations employing more than twelve million people. More than forty thousand employees were surveyed, and interviews were conducted with women of diverse identities, including women of color, members of the LGBTQ+ community identifying as women, and women with disabilities.

> Black women leaders are more likely to have colleagues question their competence and to be subjected to demeaning behavior…and 1 in 3 black women leaders say they've been denied or passed over for opportunities because of personal characteristics, including their race and gender.
>
> Latinas and Black women are less likely than women of other races and ethnicities to say their manager shows interest in their career development.
>
> Asian women and Black women are less likely to have strong allies on their teams. They are also less likely than white women to say senior colleagues have taken important sponsorship actions on their behalf, such as publicly praising their skills or advocating for a compensation increase for them. (Women in

the Workplace 2022: The Full Report, https://leanin.org/women-in-the-workplace/2022/intersectional-experiences)

These facts, currently operating and existing in workplaces of all sizes, present a disturbing reality. It's important to raise awareness of these facts, and when they can be highlighted through the examination of an individual's life and career experiences, I have an obligation to share that knowledge. I am that individual.

Amber, as you approach your twenty-fifth birthday, I thought long and hard about a memorable gift to mark this milestone. Neither of us are material girls, so I looked beyond things and tried to come up with substance. Repeatedly, I kept returning to wisdom, but I could not figure out how to pass that along. I started looking for books, and while some recommendations were desirable, they lacked *my* wisdom. It suddenly dawned on me that I could share my experience with additional guidance. What I wish I had at your age, I could create and give to you.

At the tender age of twenty-five, my role models were limited. While my family nucleus and a few cherished others provided some direction, no one could prepare me for the harsh realities of matriculating through the corporate world as an African American woman. Why was that? We did not have many examples of people of color engaging in *that* journey at that time, and if we did, they were mostly caught up in the existence of survival; they had no time to write and offer guidance for others. I often call you my soul because you get me like no one else does. Who is better to give you deeper insights into life's journey than your older soul?

The goal of this memoir is not to serve as a script; rather, it is a guide. A script requires you to follow every step as outlined with no deviation. A guide consists of recommendations for how to maneuver when you encounter similar situations. I am giving you the window and the view of my last 30 years in corporate America that you never saw. My attempt with our homelife was to shield you and show you a loving and caring mama. What I can now share with you is what Mama endured daily just to provide. While you may or may not agree with all the choices I made, I am being transparent so you can evaluate your choices rather than thinking you have to comply with everything thrown your way.

I must warn you that righteous indignation will build up in you as you read about my accounts of racism, sexism, ageism, and discrimination. Your basic instinct will be to wish the worst for all the people involved. *Do not waste your precious energy.* I have forgiven them all. No, it was not easy, but it was a burden lifted off me. Forgiveness is not just for the receiver; it is also for the giver. For me, it relieves me of the baggage others tried to dump on me and have me carry. I simply returned the baggage to the sender with a note saying, "Keep it and deal with the contents, which are your own shortcomings being projected on me." Forgiveness did not exonerate them; however, it did liberate me.

Sweet daughter, nieces, and young ladies, read and be inspired. Most of all, be informed and ready to tackle life, rather than just accepting everything that comes your way.

Guiding Principles

Everything that drowns you teaches you how to swim. Everything that cultivates you teaches you your strength. Everything that blocks you pushes you to persevere. Everything that delays you develops your patience. Everything that scares you builds your bravery. Everything that stops you shows you how to flow. Everything that leaves you frees you to level up. Everything that has made you fall empowered you to fly.

—Unknown

When I came across these golden lines, it reminded me of what this journey taught me. For every encounter, there is purpose and meaning to be gleaned. Past experiences fortify you for the next experience. The Bible reinforces this concept in Romans 5:3–5. It states, "Not only so, but we also glory in our sufferings, because we know that suffering produces perseverance; perseverance, character; and character, hope. And hope does not put us to shame, because God's love has been poured out into our hearts through the Holy Spirit, who has been given to us."

Remember the days when we had dial-up to connect to the internet? As a Gen Z baby, you learned the concept of dedicated access. Our main computer was in the basement. It was a pain because you could not do internet-related homework in your bedroom. You had to go down two flights of stairs and sit in a dedicated spot to work.

If we were in the car headed to school, it was too late if you needed additional research or wanted to make changes because you needed access to the internet source.

Over the years, we eventually gained wireless access, which allowed you to work anywhere in the house, including the outside patio. You really thought you had arrived when you got a smartphone and were truly "connected" to the source. There were no limitations once you obtained the Wi-Fi code. For me, the wireless code to balanced living is believing in and trusting God. He is all-knowing and ever-present. No Wi-Fi is needed! I can trust that He will lead and guide me to what is best for my life. I do not have to be in a church for Him to hear me. I do not have to say choice words for Him to respond. I can talk to Him as I talk to a friend. His wisdom is priceless, and I can say with confidence that He has never left me nor forsaken me. That is coverage you can count on.

Your creativity in navigating life began early. Your wit, humor, charm, and smarts never cease to amaze me. I wish it were enough, but sadly, it will not be. You need a guiding principle to lead you along the journey. I hope you enjoy how I bring *your* story into *my* story and reinforce concepts with tips, a prayer challenge, and scripture (*New International Version*). In 2 Timothy 2:16, the apostle Paul states, "All Scripture is God-breathed and is useful for teaching, rebuking, correcting, and training in righteousness." You are guaranteed a better outcome on your life's journey based on my lessons learned. May your life and career be productive and profitable as you learn from my account. May others realize and reward the wonderful talents God has blessed you with in great abundance.

HAVE A GUIDING PRINCIPLE TO CENTER YOURSELF

Power scripts

> Trust in the LORD with all your heart and lean not on your own understanding; in all your ways submit to him, and he will make your paths straight. (Proverbs 3:5–6)

> I will instruct you and teach you in the way you should go; I will counsel you with my loving eye on you. (Psalm 32:8)

> "For I know the plans I have for you," declares the LORD, "plans to prosper you and not to harm you, plans to give you hope and a future." (Jeremiah 29:11)

Personalize your prayer

Lord, be my guiding principle in life and along this career journey.

____

____

____

____

____

____

Know Your Worth and Negotiate It

I constantly knew to brace myself when it was time to pick you up from school because there would always be an adventure to go along with the school day. A normal pickup would involve me going through the car line and having them call your name to be escorted to the car. Those days were few and far between. I always entered the line with an "Amber Alert" because they would tell me to pull over to the side because one of your teachers needed to talk. In one instance, you were in the second grade and the teacher had a concern. You really loved science and would always read ahead of the assigned chapter. That was not the issue.

The problem was that you would challenge the teacher when she was teaching. You would encourage her to share more, yet that information was not part of the current lesson plan. You took it upon yourself to share more with the class than the teacher had planned to talk about. Your classmates soon began to look to you for guidance more than the teacher. The teacher was concerned she was losing her ability to lead. She asked me to pace you with the class and encourage you not to move so far ahead. I was thrilled that you were so excited about learning, and I did not adhere to the teacher's request. Shame on me, I know. The teacher eventually learned to be more creative and unite your thirst for learning with advanced work. Your early exposure to the activities of doing your research and seeking to understand a matter fully will serve you well and keep you from falling behind and being blindsided. These skills will be especially valuable in terms of negotiating your salary and work preferences.

When I first started working postgraduate school, the salary offer was high relative to what I had made before but was low relative to my peers graduating with an MBA with similar work experience. That was my first interaction with wage discrimination and how large spreads can exist for something that should be on a more level playing field. Of course, you must consider the nature of the job and the region of the country; however, after those filters were viewed, it was still clear that male salaries were higher, and White women were paid more than women of color. Sadly, it is thirty years later, and there is not much progress.

I was the first of five children to finish college and go on to graduate school. I felt so blessed to be earning double what I had made a couple of years earlier without an MBA that it never dawned on me what I was giving up by not negotiating a higher, suitable salary. My focus was on the immediate, not on the long term.

That is where the concepts of opportunity cost and compound interest come into play. What you do not get, you cannot use. You love examples, so I will illustrate: There was a $7,000 difference between my salary and those of my male peers. The simple math of not getting an additional $7,000 per year for thirty years equals $210,000. Let us take it a step further to see the opportunity cost of what I lost over the thirty years using 5 percent interest. Imagine what additional choices we would have had as a family of five with the equivalence of $495,000 more. You cannot profit from investments you do not receive.

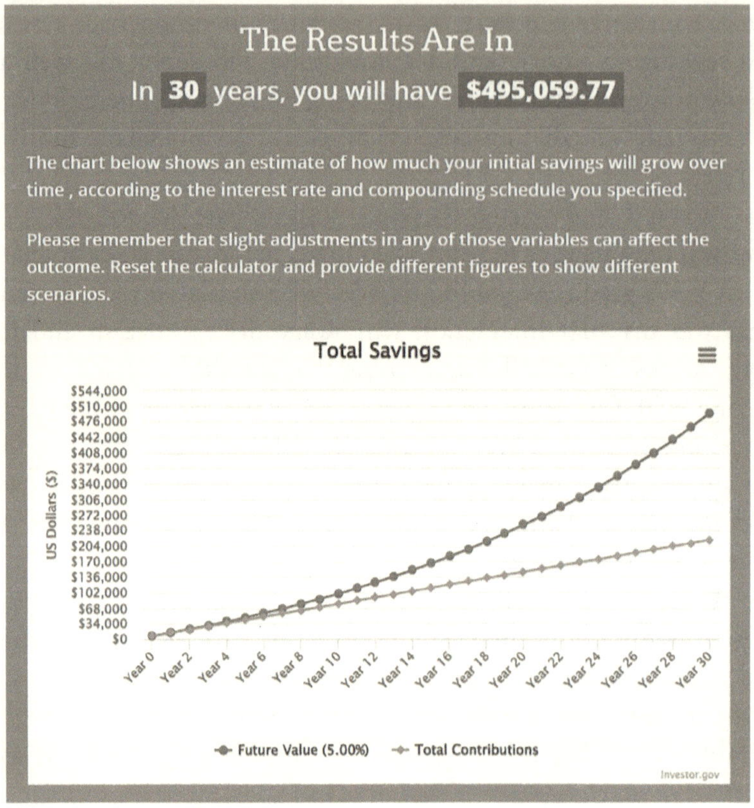

This chart was generated on investor.gov

While the concept of DEI (Diversity, Equity, and Inclusion) is the buzzword of the day, it means nothing if you do not include all three. People think they are doing you a favor if they include you. Demand more than just a seat at the table. Demand equity as well, because a seat at the table is not enough. To be whole, you must be granted the same meal to be at parity. Several websites can be leveraged to do research on specific jobs within specific regions to get a sense of the going salary rate. Closely examine salary rates and ranges. Consider browsing sites such as the following:

- ZipRecruiter.com
- LinkedIn.com
- CareerBuilder.com

- Monster.com
- Glassdoor.com
- Indeed.com
- Mynextmove.org
- Salary.com
- Payscale.com

Professional organizations in your respective field are also a valuable resource for understanding salary ranges for job types and locations.

Google has a host of great articles on negotiating your salary, and Amazon has an endless list of book recommendations on the topic.

Networking with others in the field is the most valuable source of information about the going rates. The next chapter shares more insights on networking.

A terrific book by Charles L. Karrass sums it up: *In Business as in Life, You Don't Get What You Deserve, You Get What You Negotiate.*

KNOW YOUR WORTH
AND NEGOTIATE IT

Power scripts

I praise you because I am fearfully and wonderfully made; your works are wonderful; I know that full well. (Psalm 139:14)

For we are God's handiwork, created in Christ Jesus to do good works, which God prepared in advance for us to do. (Ephesians 2:10)

But you are a chosen people, a royal priesthood, a holy nation, God's special possession, that you may declare the praises of him who called you out of darkness into his wonderful light. (1 Peter 2:9)

Personalize your prayer

Lord, help me to know my worth and negotiate it well so I am not taken advantage of.

____
____
____
____
____
____

Network and Align with Others

From the time you were exposed to four-legged pets, you wanted one. For years, you and your brothers badgered us to get a dog. Our fish were just not engaging enough for you. Your dad had been badgered into submission, but I was the one who held out. I knew from my youth that having a dog was a big responsibility, and usually, it ended up being the responsibility of the parents. "Not on my watch" was my position for many years. Little did I know that you were working with others to bring my stronghold to a halt. At the tender age of ten, you started networking with friends whose parents had caved in. You asked questions about what worked and what did not. You did research on taking care of pets and even put together a presentation. Although impressive, I was not budging. Because you are my soul and know me well, you thought of a strategy that was priceless.

At our family roundtable, you asked your dad and me to speak of fond memories of our pets. While Dad's stories were limited, I monopolized the session talking about the dog twins, Pixie and Dixie, who were forever running away until they got hungry. Nowhere else could they get a home-cooked meal instead of dry granules, so they would return home. I talked about my grandmother's dog, Spot, whom she trained to shake hands with his paw. You fell in love with the story about our terrier named Whiskers and our German shepherd named Champ. Whiskers was a little dog that would get out of the fence and terrorize the neighborhood dogs. He only did it when Champ was out of the fence as well.

After a reign of terror in the neighborhood, he would come home with a trail of dogs chasing him. Champ always stayed in the driveway because he knew what was coming. Whiskers would run to the driveway, and all the dogs trailing him would make an abrupt turn around when they saw Champ in the charge position. That is when the punch line came from you: "See, Mom, you have stories to tell. We have nothing except floating dead fish tales." That was it; you got me. What was most impressive to me was how you rallied your network to formulate your plan. You realized the strength in numbers and aggregate insight from others.

Networking is critical to your success. The saying "no man is an island" is so true. It takes a village to succeed. Someone in your network is likely to have had an experience from which you can benefit. Having a diverse network will expand both your point of view *and* your creativity. Consider the following resources during your personal journey: these advocates will help you connect, grow, and advance. Think of them as your personal TEAM.

> T—Together
> E—Everyone
> A—Achieves
> M—More

Mentor: A mentor provides guidance, advice, and feedback. Mentors are experienced and trusted advisors, often a few levels above the mentee (you) and with more tenure in the organization. A mentor helps mentees navigate the workplace.

Sponsor: A great sponsor advocates for the sponsored person (you) with the power to affect your career trajectory. From sharing network connections to proactively helping seek new opportunities within and outside the current company, sponsors are willing to use their own influence to help others further their careers. Think of this resource as a more vested mentor.

Ally: An ally is someone who supports disenfranchised and underrepresented groups of people. In some organizations, you will find intentional efforts to help those who tend to be marginalized.

Professional Associates within your respective career: Choose national, local, and African American–related organizations. The diversity of each organization will cater to your various needs.

Informal Network: Always stay connected with cherished friends and loved ones. They will be your village for all times and seasons.

Social Media: Please use this avenue responsibly. Don't use it for validation because you only see what people want you to see. Many people are fooled into thinking that likes and number of views amount to self-worth. You can run into groupthink with social media. Never lose your originality by conforming to what everyone else is doing, liking, or thinking.

Allow me to share a little about the talents God placed in me and how networking helped me to advance through a very trying situation. You will recall that in the movie *Hidden Figures*, the actress, Octavia Spencer, played the role of Dorothy Vaughan. Dorothy was a go-getter, always figuring things out. When everyone said there was no way for the IBM processing machine to work, she figured it out and made it work. She had a team of sisters that she coached and mentored. They all respected her and constantly looked to her for guidance. Her White, female manager gave her day-to-day responsibility for the management of the team but never came through with the title, position, or pay. While Dorothy respectfully challenged her manager, there was no budging on doing the right thing until Dorothy threatened to quit. The manager knew there was no suitable replacement, and she also knew the value Dorothy brought to the table. It had to come down to Dorothy taking a drastic move before the right thing was acknowledged with a proper promotion.

Fast forward to Mom. God blessed me with unique skills and tenacity. My primary role in consulting was simply figuring things out. I pray constantly for discernment in big and small matters. God never fails to hear my appeal and respond accordingly.

My generation was part of the self-service revolution, where technology advanced to the point where it could be employed to do routine tasks in a more efficient and accurate way than humans. This technology enables one to interact without requiring assistance from a service representative. I studied processes in various customer environments to understand the current operations and envision how technology could enable greater efficiencies. To build up expertise, I had to ask a lot of questions, spend a lot of time with people doing their respective jobs, and bounce ideas off others who had more experience.

Sadly, in most cases, I had to learn my job firsthand because some senior consultants, mostly White males, felt threatened. I was even told by a coworker to figure it out because I had an MBA. It is a sad realization: sometimes your advancement is a threat to others. Some people do not see a big playground. They simply focus on territory and do everything in their power to keep you from advancing. What they meant for evil, God turned around for my good. Because I had to start from nothing and learn things from beginning to end, I could speak confidently about my recommendations to a client and answer any questions that came my way.

The beauty of firsthand experience is that no one can take that away from you. *You are the expert.* That is why the Bible story in Genesis chapters 37 through 50 is my favorite. Joseph's brothers alienated him, sold him into slavery, and forgot about him. Once in Egypt, he suffered marginalization, accusations, and false imprisonment for being different. All these setbacks led to a set up for greatness. He went from slave to prisoner to second-in-command for the Egyptian head of state. That's what happens when God is in control of your destiny.

Some of the customers and technology I worked with included the following:

- Delta, American Airlines, and other major airlines to deploy the first self-check-in kiosks
- WalMart, the Home Depot, Tesco, and other top retailers with the first deployments of self-checkout

- Telcos (AT&T, Sprint, Verizon, and Rogers), deploying the first bill payment units
- US Postal Service and Pitney Bowes with their initial deployment of self-service kiosks
- Blockbuster and Redbox with their DVD rental kiosks
- Hospitals (Adventist Health Systems), clinics, and doctors' offices, deploying patient self-check-in kiosks
- Hilton and Hyatt Hotels, deploying the first guest check-in kiosks
- Hertz and Alamo with their first self-service kiosks
- International, major, regional, and community banks with their transition from envelope to image ATMs, along with the implementation of other teller automation technologies

I built an area of expertise that generated a constant stream of revenue for the company. While few people wanted to help me become an expert in my field, everyone soon wanted me to teach them everything I learned. They valued my insights and realized that the company could multiply its earnings if there were many more people doing the work. The troubling realization was this: They wanted what I worked so hard to build with no mutual benefit to me. They wanted me to dump my brain into chosen associates. What they failed to realize was the concept of anointing. When God puts an anointing on you, it cannot be "cut and pasted" elsewhere. You can share your insights, but you cannot duplicate God's impact.

In a manipulative way, my manager aligned several associates under me with the promise of a managerial position. Too often, women and minorities are *promised* a promotion to do what others are *given* a promotion to do. One thing I experienced and witnessed firsthand was the practice of women being given promises that if they performed to a particular standard, they would be given an opportunity for an advanced position. Men are often given the promotion first, with the chance to prove their worth during the process. Do not think for a second that this practice no longer exists. I am sad to report that after thirty years in corporate America, there is not much improvement in this area either.

My manager wanted me to pour into others, yet she was not vested in pouring into me. That is when I learned the value of a network. I researched the up-and-coming technology and secretly poured myself into learning it. I used my network of peers and mentors to speak on my behalf to the manager behind this innovative technology and state why I would be the best candidate to consult on their product. These advocates shared how I launched their respective products into success. It did not take much convincing because my reputation preceded me, and this manager had me on his radar. Once I had the offer in hand, I moved on without looking back. I got the promotion along with a proper team to mentor and grow. The previous manager had to disband the group because she was not competent to lead the new hires, and there was no one else with my level of expertise to help.

Networking is a valuable tool and will be a blessing to help launch and sustain you. Leverage it for simple Q and A to bounce off ideas, learn new things, and position yourself for the next move.

NETWORK AND ALIGN
WITH OTHERS

Power scripts

> Two are better than one, because they have a good return for their labor: If either of them falls, one can help the other up. But pity anyone who falls and has no one to help them up. Also, if two lie down together, they will keep warm. But how can one keep warm alone? Though one may be overpowered, two can defend themselves. A cord of three strands is not quickly broken. (Ecclesiastes 4:9–12)

> The way of fools seems right to them, but the wise listen to advice. (Proverbs 12:15)

> As iron sharpens iron, so one person sharpens another. (Proverbs 27:17)

Personalize your prayer

Lord, grant me discernment as I seek to effectively network and align with others.

____

____

____

____

Speak Up

I was always excited to pick you up from daycare. You were such a bundle of joy that I looked forward to hearing about the highlights of your day. The school's protocol was to get your bag before I connected with you because it would have a card inside with a rating system based on traffic lights that reflected the type of day you had: a red light was bad, a yellow light was okay, and green was great. I knew to prepare myself if the light was anything other than green. On this day, it was red with a note to see the teacher. I took a deep breath and braced for impact.

The teacher told me she had to put you in time-out from time to time for excessive talking. Time-out was a chair located in the corner of a room. This room's walls happened to have wallpaper with all kinds of animals. You went into time-out as required; what you did in time-out created the problem. You named the animals on the wall, and each time you were in time-out, you would greet the animals by name and talk with them! Time-out soon became a welcome part of your day because you were able to reunite with your animal friends. The teacher just threw her hands up in desperation because, in time-out, the talking continued.

Once again, I admired your ability to make the most of any situation you found yourself in. You were confident that this, too, would pass, and you created a pleasant situation out of what others would have found to be most uncomfortable. As you grew, you continued to develop the skills of resilience and talking your way out of situations. Speaking at the right time with the right message is imperative because silence gives others consent to do as they please.

You must speak up for yourself because others will try to marginalize you, talk over you, mansplain anything to you, gaslight their communication with you, and whitewash or downplay your ideas. They will try to make you feel less than able and capable. It is difficult for people to play nicely and share the playing field. The mindset of many is for you to stay in another swim lane that does not threaten theirs. They are so insecure that they cannot appreciate the diversity and value you bring when you speak up. Instead, they feel threatened by your education, experience, and confidence. The relentless push to conform is harming us. Never let anyone make you feel "less than" because you do not look like them, talk like them, go where they go, go to church the way they do, eat the food they eat, or share in the same entertainment. You are enough because God made you and put in you what He wanted you to have. Use your voice in an assertive way to exhibit confidence and speak up for yourself. You must become your own best advocate.

My clients were often White males. Rarely would I have the pleasure of sitting across the table with another person of color or even a woman. Many times, there was a rude reception and limited hospitality. I had to remind myself that I earned the right to be at the table and needed to be confident in my ability to make a difference. I was there to solve a business problem, not to win a popularity contest. Once, I was with a customer, and the reception was particularly negative. The room had twelve people: ten White males and two women. While I had the lead consultant role, I knew my message would be ignored if I did not change the delivery. It would be a long four hours otherwise. I had a White male coworker who accompanied me, and he was oblivious to what was going on. I pulled him aside and asked if he would lead the discussion. I promised to support him, and he knew I was good for it. He was more than happy because he thought the lead role should have been his anyway. Side note: It was always a struggle to get him to listen to my ideas, yet somehow, those same ideas ended up being his launching pad for solving problems. Sometimes people will not hear you just because of where the voice originates. They will not admit it to you, but they will catch your vision, latch on to the concept, and reframe it to sound original. Get used to it. It does not diminish you and simply validates your originality.

My coworker opened the meeting with the presentation I put together, and everyone thought he was a genius until the questions started. He stumbled through most questions, and I let him sweat a little before I spoke up. I answered question after question and was alright, saying that we would do additional research for those questions we did not answer in the moment. Soon enough, different members of the group asked tougher questions because they thought I was lucky to answer the initial ones. I continually answered their questions with clarity and thoroughness until soon they forgot my coworker was in the room and went deeper into the dialogue with me. I would redirect some questions to my teammate because that is what good partners do. They present a strong front and look out for each other. The meeting ended much better than it started, and I have accomplished repeat business for this client with high customer satisfaction scores. Too often, this was and still is the scenario. However, I have learned to lean in and speak up at the appropriate time with a strong message.

Some additional considerations for speaking up:

- Address issues as soon as or soon after they arise to let others know how important they are to you. If you don't respect yourself, no one else will.
- Be specific with your response to tackle the concern at hand. Your response is less effective if you address an issue that is not immediate to the situation.
- Avoid being passive-aggressive because that sends unhealthy signals. It will frustrate you because others won't take you seriously, and it will prolong you from getting to the core of the matter.
- Keep your cool because it helps you stay focused.
- Practice makes perfect. Now is a good time to start.

Be aware; you are darned if you speak up because you may get labeled as the angry Black woman when you assert yourself. You are darned if you do not speak up because you are perceived as weak with nothing of value to add. Your voice is your vocal signature. Always use it to make a positive impression.

SPEAK UP

Power scripts

> The tongue has the power of life and death, and those who love it will eat its fruit. (Proverbs 18:21)

> Those who guard their mouths and their tongues keep themselves from calamity. (Proverbs 21:23)

> There is a time for everything, and a season for every activity under the heavens: a time to be silent and a time to speak. (Ecclesiastes 3:1–8)

Personalize your prayer

Lord, fortify me with courage to speak up.

____

____

____

____

____

____

____

____

____

____

Do Your Homework

During the week, our days were routine: breakfast, drop-off at school, me heading off to work, pick up from school, homework, dinner, bath, and bed. Then we press the replay button until Friday. After one trying day at work, we went through our routine and completed the bath. I was exhausted and ready for bed. Then you remembered that you had more homework to complete, and it was rather involved. You were a star student and really cared about your grades. Because you were solid in your classes, I did not think it would be an issue to turn the homework in later. Your prior performance left you in an advantageous position to miss an assignment or turn it in later. Once you made me aware, I said, "Don't worry about it; we will deal with the consequences." Although you were concerned about the impact this would have on your grade, you agreed that it was late, and our best option now was to sleep.

To my disappointment, the next day I had to park instead of pick you up because one of the teachers needed to see me. I could not imagine what you did this time. The teacher asked me about the missing homework. She had a major attitude, and I could not imagine what was fueling it. I told her I was aware of the missing homework and told her that it was too late last night to start it and that we would turn it in later. The teacher told me she got that part of the story, and then she shared more. She stated that when she asked you about the homework, you shared that your mom said you

25

did not have to complete it last night and the teacher would have to "deal with it." My mouth dropped. Now I understood where the attitude was coming from. I told the teacher that you misunderstood my comment. Though I did say we would deal with the consequences, I did not say that the teacher had to "deal with it." We both looked at you after this discovery, and you tried to talk your way out of it. Too late! You took advantage of a situation to say what you wanted to the teacher, and your behind suffered the consequences.

Doing your homework will save you a lot of heartache. It will keep you from being blindsided. When it comes to applying for a job, know that most jobs are filled with candidates known to the hiring manager or filled by someone with the inside scoop. While some postings are legitimate, many are human resources formalities. Networking, referrals, sponsorship, and nepotism fill 50 percent of jobs.

I was excited to apply for a promotion. I had everything I needed to be successful in that position. I overheard a White female peer discuss the same job. She told another peer that she had been offered the job. When I was able to talk with her one-on-one, I asked her about the job, and she told me the hiring manager told her the job was hers. Their fathers played golf together, and he had put in a referral for her. I asked, Why would they post it if you already have the job? She answered that it helps to know people.

Unbeknownst to her, I set up some time with the hiring manager to inquire about the job. He told me to apply because I would be a great fit. He knowingly used me as a statistic to say to HR that the job was not a good fit for me, the minority candidate. The company was trying to increase its minority representation in more senior roles; therefore, the managers were encouraged to expand their applicant pool to consider more diverse candidates. I was used for HR tracking purposes, not for any true consideration. My peer, who was less qualified, got the job based on connections. That is a widespread practice, so while you are encouraged to apply for a desired position, there are many other tactics (networking, continuous learning, being results-oriented) you can deploy to position yourself to get it.

Networking: Keep connections warm through periodic check-ins. It is hard for people to connect the dots and speak up on your behalf if they have not heard from you in a long time.

Continuous Learning: Change is inevitable, so the more you keep up with what is happening in and around your field of expertise, the easier it is for you to morph into the next phase. Continuous learning helps you stay nimble and engaged. When you settle, you plateau and fail to reach your true potential. You will also get bombarded by the inner critic who tells you that you are not enough. Stay ahead of the game by keeping up and staying relevant. What is great about most organizations is that they offer certification on their dime through company education portals. They also provide access to LinkedIn Learning and other educational platforms. Take advantage of these resources to stay ahead without having to dish out the educational expenses.

Be Results-Oriented: Impact is a clear differentiator when comparing one candidate against another. Document the difference you made in your current and former roles. Making a difference means you know how to leave matters better than how you found them. Recruiters and hiring managers fatigue quickly with a laundry list of activities or attributes. What catches the eye is the impact. Your ability to make an impact speaks volumes about the value you bring. Back it up with facts and link your impact to a broader company initiative.

While it is important to give your best to your current position, you can prepare for your next role by networking, continually learning, and being results-oriented.

DO YOUR HOMEWORK

Power scripts

> The simple believe anything, but the prudent give thought to their steps. (Proverbs 14:15)

> Desire without knowledge is not good—how much more will hasty feet miss the way! (Proverbs 19:2)

> My people are destroyed from lack of knowledge. (Hosea 4:6)

Personalize your prayer

Lord, prompt me to do my homework and get fully informed on a matter.

It Is Okay to Self-Promote

Red light again? What did we do wrong? Where did this mischievous behavior come from? Your dad and I would blame each other's side of the family. If I were honest with myself, you were me on steroids, which is why I called you my soul. Thankfully, your behavior improved over time, and we could claim you without hesitation.

Little girls with long braids always seem to get the attention of the little boys among their classmates. You were no exception. To make it worse, you had beads on each braid, which caused you to stand out even more. You would get so annoyed when the boys would pull on your braids. They thought it was an act of affection, and you viewed it as pure annoyance. Your final straw was when you were on the playground trying to enjoy yourself and one of the boys pulled your braid. You picked up a handful of rocks and threw it at him. He tried to run away, but the small rocks hit him in the back. He went crying to the teacher, and you were in big trouble. That was a serious offense because more harm could have resulted. The administration called me at work to warn me of the day's events. They mentioned you could be expelled if you did it again. Not only were we embarrassed by your rash action, we were alarmed because of what could have happened.

We discussed anger management and the need to control your temper. We talked about using your words in an affirmative way when people do things you do not like. We even talked about counting to ten before you react, so you would have time to think about the consequences. For an entire week, we were elated to get green lights. You talked about things that irritated you and how you responded using the techniques. Unfortunately, the honeymoon did not last long. The day arrived when the red light returned. While I did not get a call on this one, there was a warning. I tried not to over-act when I saw you and said we would discuss it in the car. We started off talking about the good parts of the day and what went well. Then it was time to address the elephant in the room. "What made you upset today, Amber?" It was the pulling of the braids again. I said, "Please tell me you did not throw rocks."

You proudly proclaimed, "No, I did not throw rocks. I learned my lesson that rocks could hurt. I threw mulch!" All I could do was shake my head, but I was laughing inside because you counted to ten and realized the imminent danger in throwing rocks and assessed that mulch was lighter and would deter more so than harm. We discussed the option of not throwing anything and using the teacher to intervene when your words were not enough. Thankfully, that was the end of throwing things, though not the end of red lights.

It is okay to self-promote when you do an excellent job. I used to think it was bragging; however, I have come to realize that you are your best advocate. When you make a positive difference, it is okay to share the impact. It can help build your personal brand and get others to notice you for the value you bring to the table. I made the mistake year after year of not rating myself higher on performance reviews and waiting for the manager to weigh in. It is your job to document your contribution and share it at the appropriate time in a constructive way. Self-promotion can be uncomfortable; however, it is necessary.

I have held a lot of positions over the years, and each position prepared me to be more effective and well-rounded in the next role. In my early career, I moved from a financial planner role to a market-ing manager role to a product manager role. Most job descriptions identify the highlights of a role. Unless there are well-documented notes, you usually refine the role through trial and error. As a product manager, I was proud of my product launch track record and resulting market reception. I was willing to try new and innovative ways to gain traction. Some things worked better than others, and it was the willingness to operate outside of my comfort zone that brought the most benefits. As I learned more, I tweaked various aspects of the product offering to ensure market competitiveness. Soon, my manager asked me to mentor others on the team to help with the competitiveness of their offers.

Imagine my surprise when I saw a job posting with the exact same description of what I was doing in my current role, coupled with the mentoring and managing component. I scheduled a time with my manager to inquire. He said he was hiring a manager underneath him to focus on leading the product managers. I reminded him that he asked me to mentor the team because of my impact, and I would be interested in applying for the position. He shared with me that he did not feel I had advanced in maturity to oversee others in the manager role, and he did want me to train the new manager he hired. Wait! Did he even think about what he just asked me? Yes, I had the stare plus the head tilt, like, *What did you just say?* My inner thought was, *I am good enough to* do *the job but not good enough to* have *the job.*

My manager ended up bringing in one of his friends from outside the company, and he was ill-equipped to lead the team. He did not have the skill set nor the background to be a proper fit. It was evident early on that the team would suffer under this new manager, and I simply refused to be a part of it. I moved on to a new role within weeks. The new manager did not last a year. The company had to intervene because the business began to suffer under his tenure.

My failure to have a trail of documentation of my capabilities was part of the reason I was not taken seriously with my appeal to be manager. I should have created more documentation and would have had more leverage to challenge authority when I was told I was not qualified. I should not have waited for someone else to put my accomplishments in writing. That was for me to document and draw upon when needed.

What people do not know about you, they cannot recognize or acknowledge. I have since learned to document my impact and ensure that it gets referenced everywhere it can—periodic reviews with my manager, during quarterly and annual performance reviews, featured on my resume, posted on my social media and professional site, within industry articles, listed on my profile with professional associations, etc. I no longer wait for others to speak on my behalf. I self-promote in appropriate ways.

Self-promotion is not always what you say about yourself; it can also show up in what you do. Raising your hand to take the lead on a project, suggesting ways that current processes can be enhanced, and taking the lead on implementing improvements without being requested are all ways to showcase your ability.

To whom you promote yourself is as important as what you promote about yourself. Target those who have influence, managerial authority, and impact over your career path.

While it is good to self-promote, it is nauseating to others to hear you brag. There is a delicate balance between the two. Here is what *not* to do:

- Do not lie about your accomplishments. The truth will eventually be discovered.
- Do not try to be a copycat of someone who is getting attention. Be authentic. No one can be the unique person God made you to be. Be the best you and not a good substitute for someone else. Focus on what is unique about *your* accomplishments.
- Keep it relevant. While there is no need to share everything, do be prepared to share what is important and significant. How did your participation add value to the solution?

Examine yourself and embrace what is unique about you. Share that goodness with others strategically and often.

IT IS OKAY TO SELF-PROMOTE

Power scripts

Always be prepared to give an answer to everyone who asks you to give the reason for the hope that you have. But do this with gentleness and respect. (1 Peter 3:15–16)

For I will give you words and wisdom that none of your adversaries will be able to resist or contradict. (Luke 21:15)

Each one should test their own actions. Then they can take pride in themselves alone, without comparing themselves to someone else. (Galatians 6:4)

Personalize your prayer

Lord, instruct me on the areas I need to self-promote and avenues to do it.

____
____
____
____
____
____
____
____

Do Not Take No for an Answer

Dinnertime was always a wind-down period for the day. The adventures of the day were all dealt with, and it was time for the family to reconnect and share each other's company. Sometimes, dinnertime would turn tense when you or your brothers would drink first and not leave room for food. We worked too hard to waste anything, especially food. To combat that issue, Dad made a rule that you had to drink after you ate. That worked for a while until creativity entered your thoughts. Your cup had a built-in straw. During this meal, you asked Dad if you could take a sip. You were doing so well with the meal that he agreed to allow you to take a sip.

One small sip led to a long sip until all your juice was gone. Dad was livid. He headed to our trusty storage for the wooden spoon. You were in for it, and Dad was going to punish you for disobedience. Once again, I found myself as your intercessor. I pulled Dad aside and told him that technically, he gave you permission to sip and did not put parameters around it. After a tense exchange, he agreed to not spank you but instead punish you and clearly state the rules of sipping. Who knew we had to add rules to the rules? Once again, your creativity had you dig deep for a solution that would satisfy your desire. You managed to find a way when the obvious way was cut off. You did not take no for an answer.

Standing your ground is necessary in some scenarios because your reputation may be at stake. The truth cannot prevail if you do not reveal it. Your reputation cannot be defended if you do not speak up. Not speaking up is not an option. You simply cannot take no for an answer when you must act.

The business of consulting is very complimentary to our hardware and software business because the more a client understands the value of technology in their environment, the more they are willing to invest. Clients invest more when they understand not just what it is they are buying but also why and how that technology can have an influence. When a client can speak confidently to their superiors and key stakeholders regarding the return on investment of their purchase, it is more evident that you have done your job as a consultant because the client is the one who must live with the decisions made. They must defend the purchase long after you are gone. So, in business, the consulting group is very complimentary to the technology group.

As manager of the consulting team, I met with the senior leaders of the technology business to review our business plan annually and illustrate how we were an enabler to their business. The more our plans were connected, the better we could operate as an organization. My senior vice president (SVP) wanted to review the plan with me prior to presenting. I felt confident in the business plan and was ready to present, yet I took no exception to meeting with my superior because she could add another pair of lenses to the plans. She also knew the pulse of her peers and could provide feedback that was useful in the delivery of the message.

We had about three weeks until the presentation, and I tried several times to get on her agenda, but something was always more important. Therefore, we never met prior to meeting with the senior vice president of the technology group. All the participants in the meeting were at the VP or senior VP level, and none looked like me in terms of nationality or gender. My SVP was a woman; that was all we had in common. She had a limited window into my world and no desire to learn more. Prior to the start of the meeting, she pulled me aside and expressed her annoyance that I did not make more of an effort to get on her agenda. Although I tried on multiple occasions and even sent her the presentation in advance, she failed to review it. Somehow, it was my oversight.

Once all the participants arrived and the pleasantries were completed, I was asked to present. Before I could speak, my SVP spoke up and expressed concern that she did not get a chance to review in advance, so she could not cosign on the plan. She suggested we move on to another agenda item, and we would follow up later. My heart sank because she did not have to start the meeting off like that. I felt thrown under the bus, run over by the front wheel, and dragged several miles. Everything in me wanted to launch across the table and pop her in the mouth. I thank God for putting dignity in me and answering my short and specific prayer: Lord, help me to hold out! A voice in my head said, *You got this*, so I spoke up and said, "No, I am prepared to present, and let us move on," in an affirmative voice. I acknowledged to the group that I was open to candid feedback and would apply any adjustments that were deemed necessary. I purposely did not look in her direction because she had been enough of a distraction.

I went through several slides and delivered a powerful and credible plan. I was able to confidently answer every question posed. At the end of the presentation, the technology SVP and his team were blown away. He acknowledged that the plan was well thought out and clearly outlined the link between how consulting would accelerate his business. During the presentation, I showed my organization chart, and it had an open slot because I needed to hire for a specific role. The technology SVP made a joke that he had done similar work in his previous company and would be honored to apply for the job. I responded with a smile and said that if I could afford him, I would consider him for the role. It was a great ending to a very productive meeting. My SVP had the nerve to chime in and say, "We always come through."

We, I thought. Who is *we*? Are we French now? You disowned me, and now you want to claim me? In my mind, I was thinking, *Lady, do you see the tire tracks I have on my suit because you threw me under the bus? God made it into a pinstriped pattern, and I am standing proudly representing* Him, *not you.*

By not taking no for an answer, you tip the scale on what is possible and what is not. Go for what you know is right.

DO NOT TAKE NO FOR AN ANSWER

Power scripts

> I keep my eyes always on the LORD. With him at my right hand, I will not be shaken. (Psalm 16:8)

> Let us not become weary in doing good, for at the proper time we will reap a harvest if we do not give up. (Galatians 6:9)

> You need to persevere so that when you have done the will of God, you will receive what he has promised. (Hebrews 10:36)

Personalize your prayer

Lord, grant me the serenity to accept the things I cannot change and direction on the areas where I should not take no for an answer.

CHAPTER 9

Be Authentic

When you got in the car after school, you would hear one of two songs, and that gave you insight into the course of my day.

> I'm safe and sound
> Serene and calm
> Whenever I'm here, I know you're with me
> My secret place
> Where I escape
> From all the cares of this race
> Because of your grace.
> (CeCe Winans, "Alone in His Presence")

or

> Y'all gon' make me lose my mind
> up in HERE, up in here
> Y'all gon' make me go all out
> up in here, up in here
> Y'all gon' make me act a FOOL
> up in HERE, up in here
> Y'all gon' make me lose my cool
> up in here, up in here.
> (DMX, "Party Up [Up in Here]")

If you heard CeCe, it was a wonderful day, and I was leaving the throne room with the sound of birdies tweeting all around. All was well with the world.

When you heard DMX, it was one of those hectic days. It took every fiber of my being to keep it together.

For many years, there were more DMX days than CeCe days. I felt challenged constantly because I struggled to assimilate in the corporate world, which was hell-bent on keeping me out or forcing me to conform to its norms. Anything not fitting the mold came under intense scrutiny. My authentic self was compromised in the shuffle. While I never lowered my moral standard, I compromised too much. From hair to dress to music to events to sports to social activities, promotions took place in *their* circles of comfort, and I wanted to advance. I suppressed my ideas and aspirations so others would not feel threatened. I did what I thought was necessary to be part of the team and make others comfortable.

In the age of *patriotism*, we are bombarded with messages about America the Great—that great nation that is home to the free and the brave. Are we not one nation, under God, indivisible, with liberty and justice for all? So how is it that we are so far from God's ideal for this nation? In this Bible-believing nation, has anyone really read and embraced what God Himself has declared in Romans 2:11: "For God does not show favoritism." In His eyes, there are no superior people. While God does outline the characteristics of His chosen people, He never promotes a race or gender that supersedes others. The mentality in America has not caught up to this truth. It's our way or the highway.

The irony of life today is that you are encouraged to be your authentic self while everything around you markets efforts to conform. At work, innovation is encouraged, though if you think outside the box, you get told to bring it down to earth and stay in the realistic zone. Social media influencers tell you what you should wear, how you should speak, what you should eat and drink, how you should look, what is the most watched movie you should watch, what to read, and even who to be with based on your zodiac sign.

Originality has no place in our conformist society. When you stand out, you are accused of going against the norm. Who gave someone else the authority to set my norm or direct my true north? Why am I considered the outlier when I think for myself and make decisions based on sound logic, knowledge, and understanding? It took years before I realized that I was okay. Many challenges I faced in corporate America were not because I was a problem but because I failed to conform. God made me an individual, and I have finally come to terms with how to live accordingly.

The journey toward authenticity is a lifelong process. It requires self-evaluation and looking at the reason behind what we do. You must be intentional in evaluating your values, options, and actions. When we live more authentically, we have confidence, strength, individuality, and emotional resilience.

One area of compromise was our hair. Every six weeks, it was time for the creamy crack. The growing hair roots would always inform us that it was time for our touch-up perm. I never understood why they called it perm if you must keep getting the relaxer. They should call it what it is: a temporary straightener. Like clockwork, we subjected ourselves to the ritual—greasing the edges and scalp, hoping not to burn, and then sitting for twenty minutes while the perm did its magic. The result was straightened hair that made us look "normal." The problem is, we bought into that rhetoric, or, should I say, I bought into that rhetoric and imposed it on you. Authenticity is about staying true to yourself. I compromised in many areas because I wanted to assimilate and not be different. I had to make others feel comfortable with me, and all the while not being comfortable with myself.

A turning point for us both happened as we watched the movie, *Good Hair* which was produced by Chris Rock. It forced us to face up to the fact that we were trying so hard to assimilate. It was yet another area of compromise. It was not because we lacked something others had; rather, it was because we did not want to seem different. Once we learned the hazards of the chemicals we were exposed to, we both committed to going natural. After 14 years, neither of us regretted that decision. We gave ourselves permission to wear braids, twists, locs, afro puffs, hot comb–straightened tresses, bantu knots, whatever suits our hearts' content.

Authenticity is core to your well-being. In her book, *The Authenticity Principle*, Ritu Basin sums up what it means to be your authentic self: "Resist Conformity, Embrace Differences, and Transform How You Live, Work, and Lead." Our next chapter focuses more on understanding, challenging, and appreciating yourself. Never forget, God made no mistake in making you—everything about you is unique, should be appreciated, and should be celebrated.

BE AUTHENTIC

Power scripts

> Before I formed you in the womb I knew you, before you were born I set you apart. (Jeremiah 1:5)

> And even the very hairs of your head are all numbered. (Matthew 10:30)

> Follow God's example, therefore, as dearly loved children. (Ephesians 5:1)

Personalize your prayer

Lord, you made me original, and I need help in this conformist world to be true to my authentic self.

CHAPTER 10

Treat Yo Self

Audrey Hepburn was one of my favorite actresses growing up. She had so much style and class. Her movie, *Breakfast at Tiffany's,* revealed a world that was so far removed from my reality as a child. I was a Grady baby. That was considered the place where the poorest people in Atlanta were born. It was one of the only places that African Americans could go for healthcare in Atlanta. My upbringing took place in a modest and humble home. Extravagance came only from TV and imagination. The main scene in the movie focused on Audrey's character all dressed up at the most elegant jewelry store in Manhattan. She, along with everyone around her, looked like they walked out of *Vogue* magazine. Everything about them said classy: dress, hair, clothing, jewelry, and attitude.

That scene came back to mind during one of my business trips. I had a speaking engagement in Orlando, Florida, at the Waldorf Astoria, a high-end Hilton property. It was in December, and all the Christmas decor was top-notch. The entire property was filled with white lights and Christmas trees. The service was first-class, and the rooms were designed for royalty. During this trip, you and my mom accompanied me. It was so cool to have you all tag along on trips because I could expose you to a world I only dreamed about as a kid. While I was busy at work, you two would explore the property and make great memories.

On one of the conference days, I stopped in during lunch to check on you both. You had just returned from brunch and were stuffed. You had a plate of pastries on the counter for me to try. The chef had come out to your table and asked how you were enjoying your meal. My mom was a professional cook and shared how tasty the food was. You were only about eight, but you chimed in to tell him what an excellent job he did. You shared with the chef your favorite treat and asked if he had more like it. He sent a sample of treats to the table, and you and Mom finished the meal and returned to the room. I had to admit that the pastries were second to none.

It was not until we checked out of the hotel that I realized we paid a hefty price for that brunch and extra for the pastries. I had given Mom my credit card to cover all your food expenses. Because it was a work trip, I needed to keep personal expenses separate from work expenses. I was blown away by the price of that brunch. It was more than a week's grocery trip for the entire family. When I mentioned the cost to you, you did not understand the problem. You reminded me that I gave Mom the credit card and told her to "treat yo self to brunch." Your mind was stuck on the *Parks and Recreation* episode where Tom and Donna talked about their once-a-year spending spree and treating themselves to the best of the best of everything. I had to explain to you and Mom the difference between a figurative term and a literal term.

Treating yourself to extra attention is necessary in this dog-eat-dog world because we are fragile individuals that need to be fortified. Otherwise, we will easily succumb to life's pressures. It is never a question about whether you will encounter pressure. It is a question of when it is coming and how much. Life is a great balancing act, and when one part of your existence is out of balance, it impacts the whole. Let us talk about the various parts that make up the whole of you and what you can do to treat yo self to balance in physical health, mental health, emotional health, financial health, moral health, and spiritual health.

Physical health is influenced by our habits, routines, and behaviors. Be mindful of how you take care of yourself. "An ounce of prevention is worth a pound of cure" is used to mean that it is better and easier to stop a problem from happening than to correct it *after* it has started. In the book *Something to Shout About,* Donna Green-Goodman highlights the *best way* to take care of yourself.

B	Bedtime Regularity	Come to me, all you who are weary and burdened, and I will give you rest. (Matthew 11:28)
E	Exercise	In the name of Jesus Christ of Nazareth, walk. (Acts 3:6)
S	Sunshine and Simple Diet	But for you who revere my name, the sun of righteousness will rise with healing in its rays. And you will go out and frolic like well-fed calves. (Malachi 4:2) Then God said, "I give you every seed-bearing plant on the face of the whole earth and every tree that has fruit with seed in it. They will be yours for food." (Genesis 1:29)
T	Temperance	Everyone who competes in the games goes into strict training. They do it to get a crown that will not last, but we do it to get a crown that will last forever. (1 Corinthians 9:25)
W	Water	Let the one who is thirsty come; and let the one who wishes take the free gift of the water of life. (Revelation 22:17)
A	Air	Then the LORD God formed a man from the dust of the ground and breathed into his nostrils the breath of life, and the man became a living being. (Genesis 2:7)
Y	Yielding to Divine Power	"For I know the plans I have for you," declares the LORD, "plans to prosper you and not to harm you, plans to give you hope and a future." (Jeremiah 29:11)

In the magazine *Amazing Health Facts: 8 Bible Secrets for a Longer and Stronger Life!* Doug Batchelor provides details on each one of these areas.

According to the CDC, "*Mental health* includes our emotional, psychological, and social well-being. It affects how we think, feel, and act. It also helps determine how we manage stress, relate to others, and make healthy choices." Most reputable companies have an Employee Assistance Program (EAP) that you can take advantage of to connect to resources and therapists. This is a free service. Never be ashamed to treat yo self to mental well-being.

Emotional health is different from mental health because it incorporates overall well-being. When you are in good emotional health, it does not mean you are perpetually happy and free from negative emotions. It does mean you have the skills and resources to manage the difficulties of day-to-day living. Good emotional health is reflected in resilience to stress, stronger relationships, higher self-esteem, and more energy. I am reinforcing some of the areas you witnessed me pursue to keep it together. Make sure you have plenty of options for yourself.

meditation	journaling	listening to music	talking to a therapist
exercise	being authentic	social interaction	quality sleep
shopping	spa day	road trip	eating out
brain games	gardening	reading	movies
church	picnic	concert	camping

Financial health considers fiscal things such as your income, debts, expenses, and savings and provides a snapshot of your financial situation. We work too hard not to give an account of everything that we earn. You want your money to work as hard for you as you work for it. A certified financial planner can help you with professional management of your funds, and you can manage the day-to-day expenses by utilizing a monthly budget to control the cash ins and outs. Prioritize needs versus wants to minimize impulsive spending. Start saving early to take advantage of compound interest and security.

Moral health involves making decisions, taking actions that align with your values and beliefs, and being committed to personal growth, accountability, and development. Sex with a coworker for gain, cheating on your expense reports, lying about people to appear more favorable, overbilling the customer for work not accomplished, taking a Netflix binge during working hours, using sick time to do your own thing, and disliking other humans because they differ from you are real moral dilemmas you will face daily. Guiding principles will help you tip the scale toward respectable behavior.

Spiritual health is a combination of all the areas of health in that it incorporates the guiding principles of your life and centers everything you do to align with what you believe. Colossians 3:17 says, "And whatever you do, whether in word or deed, do it all in the name of the Lord Jesus, giving thanks to God the Father through him."

To succeed in your career, you must bring your whole self to work. Everything that is going on in areas outside of work will impact you for the better or for the worse.

TREAT YO SELF

Power scripts

Take delight in the LORD, and he will give you the desires of your heart. (Psalm 37:4)

A cheerful heart is good medicine, but a crushed spirit dries up the bones. (Proverbs 17:22)

But seek first his kingdom and his righteousness, and all these things will be given to you as well. (Matthew 6:33)

Personalize your prayer

Lord, help me to be in tune with my whole self and honor this precious vessel You made me to be.

Be Prepared to Act

During your high school years, we were elated that you were part of the oratory team. It was a perfect match for your quick wit, speaking, and acting skills. Your gift of gab finally met its match. You had the unique ability to morph in and out of characters. Our favorite presentation was *One Big Happy Family*. The teacher in that story was exasperated with the unique nature of each student. You had to change into different postures as you spoke to each student during their spring performance. You nailed it each time you performed it. Your drama coach was a great advocate and ensured you received plenty of opportunities to compete in various contests. That performance won you so many awards and even a collegiate scholarship. Each award you earned elevated you to new heights—city-, district-, and state-level championships.

It was at the state tournament that you competed against the best of the best from each of their respective district competitions. The finals were held at a very conservative college with little to no representation of other nationalities. While some people told you that you were out of your league, we encouraged you to perform at your peak. You earned the right, like everyone else, to be on that stage. Just because you did not look like anyone else, in no way did it diminish your talents.

It was a grueling three-day event. The competition started with more than a hundred participants representing various categories.

During the final half-day, the contestant list in your category of humorous interpretation dwindled down to a handful of short-listed participants. They were all vying for the state's top three places. You took the stage and owned every moment of your final presentation. At its conclusion, everyone in the audience stood up and gave you a standing ovation. We were so proud of you for going the distance. When it was time to announce the winners, everyone was on edge. While we knew your performance was excellent, we also had reservations. You were the only performer of color, and there had never been a person of color to win. That should not have mattered, but we were not living in fantasyland. We were hopeful that the judges would do the right thing and extend the awards based on merit.

The third-place winner was awarded, and it was not you. The second-place winner was awarded, and it was not you. The judge announced that, for the first time in the history of the competition, they had a tie for first place. They announced you and a White male. While we were ecstatic about your win, we were also confused about the tie. The crowd booed the decision and chanted your name. Even your program director, a White woman, was confused. She did not know how to verbalize the discrepancy. Your dad and I knew the deal but did not want to call it what it was because people were waiting on us to use the race card. I really appreciate the next step your program director took. She was prepared to act. She requested the judges provide her with the scoring sheets.

Imagine our surprise when we discovered your score was higher than the White male who "tied" with you. Your director was furious, but the judges insisted that the commentary on his scorecard plus his scores was considered suitable for your commentary and higher score. Even Krusty the Clown knew that was pure rubbish. It did not bother you much because you were still awarded a first-place medal and trophy. The school was proud to get their name on the map and to have the bragging rights of a first-place winner.

Our hearts were left with mixed emotions because we realized that the toxic world would not wait until you were an adult before it imposed racism on you. We hated that you and your siblings would have to navigate an unfair system, and we could not always be there to act as your buffer.

At the pinnacle of my career, I led an organization of top-notch professionals. It was like running a small organization, which included people supervision, P&L management, client relations, selling, marketing, expense control, and project management. I was thrilled to be considered a trusted adviser within and outside the company. As I settled into my role, it became clear to me that there were disparities in pay between coworkers. My salary offer to lead the same group was less than the two males who preceded me. To make matters worse, some of the team members made more than me, and that made no sense. I had significantly more responsibility for managing the team, and they were all individual contributors. Neither of the previous managers operated in a scenario where the associates they managed were paid more than them.

I brought my concerns to Human Resources (HR). My concerns fell on deaf ears. I was the one who was talked down to, as if I should just shut up and accept the fact that I was a highly compensated individual. It should never have been about what I was being paid; rather, it should have been about what I was *not* being paid because of my worth, leadership, and organizational role that they were more than willing to pay the males who previously held the role. I thought HR was supposed to serve as associate advocates, but they aligned with management in dismissing my claims, even though the evidence for further investigation was clear.

"When they go low, we go high" is the phrase made famous by Michelle Obama. Michelle explained that "going high" means not stooping to the level of bullies or those who are cruel. It means taking the high road and not resorting to the same tactics as those who are attacking you. There was a daily battle inside me to stick it to them and take the path of least resistance to get my work done. However, my personal values reminded me to show up each day to work for men as if I were working for God. I could have easily walked away and provided my talents to a worthy organization. Unfortunately, leaving would leave the problem intact. I felt it was necessary to stand up for all those who had been marginalized over the years, those who were currently in similar situations, and those who would encounter this situation if the company were not made to face up to its demons.

When I could not get anyone in the company to champion my cause, I acted on my own behalf. I contacted an attorney's office, and the legal team agreed to support me in the effort to gain parity in compensation. They sent several letters to management, and each time it was met with an illogical, gaslighting, mansplaining response. Unfortunately, we had to involve the Equal Employment Opportunity Commission (EEOC). While that was not the way I intended to end my career, I refused to sit down and swallow injustice. It is a bitter pill that no one should ingest.

Injustice and marginalization have impacts that affect the person targeted and those around them.

- I was viewed as inferior in the eyes of others in the organization. People really get caught up on titles, and when they see that disparity, they treat you accordingly.
- My flexibility in recognizing people on the team was limited. They had to leave the team to grow in salary. I could not award them more because I was not being paid more.
- I was unable to bring in higher-caliber talent from the outside because my salary did not allow for much flexibility.

While the outcome of my case is in God's hands through the legal process, I acted and have no regrets. I felt compelled to act because of the following:

1. *Silence is equivalent to approval.* People are empowered to continue down a specific track if they are not challenged. Even if they do not change, they will not forget the role you played by speaking up. You can ignore the truth, but you cannot forget it.
2. *Others will benefit from my speaking out.* It would be a selfish act on my part if I did not speak up and try to make a difference for those who are in a similar situation or for those who come after me.

3. *It creates a paper trail.* The issue of discrimination and pay parity has now surfaced and will surface again. If I have documented my grievance, it has a history, and no one wants to be on the wrong side of history. They will think twice when a comparable situation occurs.

You (David) will feel at a disadvantage being the underdog when fighting the giant (Goliath). If you are unfamiliar with the story, you can read it in 1 Samuel 17. Realize that you do have advantages. David was fueled by faith. When you have an anchor, you are empowered. You have a history that has prepared you for the present. Past victories are bridges to larger victories. When positioning himself to fight on behalf of the kingdom, David told of his accounts of killing a lion and a bear to protect his sheep. Those encounters were building blocks. David had the advantage of looking up. He kept his lens focused on the target. Goliath approached David with arrogance. He let his guard down and took off his helmet. He was looking down, and that gave David the line of sight he needed to aim the stone at his forehead. David took his one shot and defeated the enemy.

As John Lewis has suggested, sometimes you need to get in "good trouble, necessary trouble" to make a difference. Life will present many opportunities to step up for meaningful change. You must not be afraid; rather, be prepared to act.

BE PREPARED TO ACT

Power scripts

Speak up for those who cannot speak for themselves, for the rights of all who are destitute. Speak up and judge fairly; defend the rights of the poor and needy. (Proverbs 31:8–9)

Learn to do right; seek justice. Defend the oppressed. Take up the cause of the fatherless; plead the case of the widow. (Isaiah 1:17)

Shout it aloud, do not hold back. Raise your voice like a trumpet. Declare to my people their rebellion. (Isaiah 58:1)

Personalize your prayer

Lord, grant me courage as I face negative forces that need to be dealt with, and help me to be prepared to act.

____

____

____

____

____

____

____

____

____

Above All, Get Wisdom

As mentioned in the introduction to this book, my wish for you is wisdom. It is the most important thing in life to pursue. While it is not an elusive treasure, it is one that is readily provided. The Bible's book of Proverbs is filled with golden nuggets about wisdom. It will start to transform your life in a positive way when you pursue its lessons.

Wisdom does require obedience. It is not enough to just read and listen to instructions. To avoid mayhem, you must follow the guidelines. The book of Proverbs has 31 chapters. I challenge you to read a chapter each day of the month and contemplate the goodness. Wisdom will lead, guide, preserve, and enhance your life.

Let us take a journey back to grade school and go through the what, why, when, how, and where of wisdom.

What is wisdom? According to Wikipedia, wisdom is "the ability to contemplate and act productively using knowledge, experience, understanding, common sense, and insight." True wisdom is the ability to do and say what God would do and say in every situation—the ability to see life from a divine vantage point.

> To God belong wisdom and power; counsel
> and understanding are His. (Job 12:13)

Why is wisdom important? Common sense, or instinct, is not enough to go on.

> There is a way that appears to be right, but
> in the end, it leads to death. (Proverbs 14:12)

Wisdom adds years to your life.

> For through wisdom your days will be many,
> and years will be added to your life. (Proverbs
> 9:11)

When is wisdom beneficial? Wisdom helps you understand who your friends really are.

> Wisdom will save you from the ways of
> wicked men, from men whose words are per-
> verse. (Proverbs 2:12)

Wisdom is the source of promotion and wealth. Wisdom in these verses is referred to as a she. I love that part (smile).

> Long life is in her right hand; in her left
> hand are riches and honor. (Proverbs 3:16)
> Cherish her, and she will exalt you; embrace
> her, and she will honor you. (Proverbs 4:8)

Wisdom shows you how to manage your emotions.

> Fools give full vent to their rage, but the
> wise bring calm in the end. (Proverbs 29:11)

How do I acquire wisdom? Consent to wisdom; do not resist it, or you will suffer a negative outcome.

But since you refuse to listen when I call and no one pays attention when I stretch out my hand, since you disregard all my advice and do not accept my rebuke, I in turn will laugh when disaster strikes you; I will mock when calamity overtakes you—when calamity overtakes you like a storm, when disaster sweeps over you like a whirlwind, when distress and trouble overwhelm you. Then they will call to me, but I will not answer; they will look for me but will not find me. (Proverbs 1:24–28)

Where does wisdom have influence? By imitating the wise and learning from the foolish.

Walk with the wise and become wise, for a companion of fools suffers harm. (Proverbs 13:20)

When a mocker is punished, the simple gain wisdom; by paying attention to the wise they get knowledge. (Proverbs 21:11)

ABOVE ALL, GET WISDOM

Power scripts

For the LORD gives wisdom; from His mouth come knowledge and understanding. (Proverbs 2:6)

Do not forsake wisdom, and she will protect you; love her, and she will watch over you. The beginning of wisdom is this: Get wisdom. Though it cost all you have, get understanding. (Proverbs 4:6, 7)

If any of you lacks wisdom, you should ask God, who gives generously to all without finding fault, and it will be given to you. (James 1:5)

Personalize your prayer

Lord, humble me to receive Your wisdom and grant understanding in all areas of my life.

____
____
____
____
____
____
____
____

People Will Talk

I am always amazed at how other people are quick to label you as successful or not. They will measure you against their standards of success: riches, recognition, position, and possessions. Even Merriam-Webster defines *success* as "the attainment of fame, wealth, or social statuses." Ultimately, true success is not equivalent to a position. It is not even measured by the amount of money you make. It is not in the title. It is not in the number of people you manage or the millions you produce. It is understood that those things are important to some degree, yet they have an expiration date. You cannot take them to the grave. You spend more time keeping others from trying to get them than simply enjoying them. Success is a state of being.

Success for me has three components:

- Understanding and aligning your life with the purpose God set for you
- Making a positive difference in the world around you
- Raising the bar from where you started and setting a standard for those who will follow

Align these principles with your definition of success, or you will always try to measure up to what others expect you to be, and it will drive you mad. You will never measure up to an outsider's standard because it is not a personal standard. Be sure to calibrate it from time to time to keep it fresh and relevant. That way, when people try to marginalize your success, you can go back to your definition and use a proper scale of measurement.

People will talk about you. If it is positive, make sure there is plenty of evidence to back it up. If what they say about you is negative, make sure there is plenty of evidence to refute it.

When I reached the milestone of thirty years with the company, my story was featured during Black History Month. I would like to share with you what was written, along with a handful of comments from those who read it. I only selected a few posts because it would take another chapter to log all the feedback. My heart was overjoyed with how my peers responded.

* * * * *

Meet Faye Irving, Banking Transformation Practice Leader

Faye Irving's commitment to customer dedication has been evident over the course of her 30-year career at the company. Having worked in many roles across various organizations within the company, Faye has been able to impact not only her customers, but her fellow employees. The Black Alliance has witnessed that impact firsthand through her commitment to our mission and vision, and her desire to make a difference to the local and global community through her extensive volunteer work. We spoke with Faye to discuss her career, her volunteer work and the importance of diversity, equity, and inclusion.

Could you begin with a brief overview of your background and journey to the company?

- *When I was an MBA student at Purdue University, the company sponsored our computer lab and student programming, similar to the partnership that now exists with Georgia Tech. I was convinced the company understood technology and the wave of the future. I started as a Financial Analyst reporting the results. It was too mundane for me to just report on results and not be a part of generating the results. From Financial Planning, my career path led me to Product Management (developing the offers), Marketing (promoting the offers), Pre Sales (selling the offers) and Business Consulting (delivering the offers).*

What makes you want to stay at the Company?

As you can see from my myriad of assignments over the last 30 years, what makes me want to stay is the opportunity to constantly advance my skill set to provide more value to my clients. I have been fortunate to assist leading organizations in their transformation efforts. Some early customer engagements included:

- *Delta, American Airlines, and other major airlines to deploy the first self-check-in kiosks*
- *Wal-Mart, The Home Depot, Tesco, and other top retailers with the first deployments of self-checkout*
- *Telcos (AT&T, Sprint, Verizon, & Rogers) deploying the first bill payment units*
- *U.S. Postal Service and Pitney Bowes with their initial deployment of self-service kiosks*
- *Blockbuster and Redbox with their DVD rental kiosks*
- *Hospitals (Adventist Health Systems), clinics, and doctors' offices, deploying patient self-check-in kiosks*
- *Hilton and Hyatt Hotels deploying the first guest check-in kiosks*
- *Hertz and Alamo with their first self-service kiosks*
- *International, major, regional, and community banks with their transition from envelope to image ATMs, along with the implementation of other Teller Automation Technologies (i.e., TCR/TCD, Interactive Teller, and Interactive Banker)*

I love the cross-Industry environment where I can take a base level of skills and apply them anywhere.

**What inspires you the most in your work? What
do you love the most about your role?**

- *My favorite quote is "Leadership is about making others better as a result of your presence and making sure that impact lasts in your absence." My clients trust me to help solve difficult challenges. They know I don't always have the immediate answer, but they do know I have their best interest at heart, and I will exhaust all resources to find an innovative solution to advance their efforts.*
- *What I love the most about my role is that every day is another opportunity to learn, grow, and contribute.*

**What advice would you give someone just
starting their career at the company?**

- *Challenge yourself constantly because when you don't, you will plateau and someone else will excel where you were meant to be. One of my favorite exercises is yoga. What appears so easy turns out to be a challenging set of flows. Now I look forward to more advanced routines.*

**Outside of work, where can we most likely find
you or what are you most often doing?**

- *I really enjoy volunteer work. With the company, I have had the opportunity to lead and participate in the annual Susan B. Komen Breast Cancer Fundraiser, Technology Recycling donations, Boulevard Shelter Thanksgiving and Christmas donation collections, CURE - Laurens Run for Children's Cancer, Junior Achievement, Salvation Army Girls and Boys Club campus refresh project, and the latest MLK Day 2022 work on the watershed trail. What an incredible benefit to live your passion and do your job at the same place.*

Is there anything specific that you have learned through your support of local organizations and your global volunteer efforts that are most important to you? What impacts your life the most?

- *My passion is education access for all. I love going around the world building infrastructures for those who don't have access. I truly believe education is a right all should have access to because when you know better, you do better. Last year, I was featured on the cover of Maranatha International for some work we did in building a remote school extension in Zambia, Africa. Through this organization, I have also completed construction projects in Peru, Bolivia, India, Côte d'Ivoire, Africa, and two separate trips to Kenya.*

As we focus on diversity, I'm curious what would you love to continue seeing within the company pertaining to diversity and inclusion?

- *The current team I manage consists of 20 individuals representing 12 separate nationalities, and our combined creativity is second to none. I would love to see the company continue to grow to look more like its customer base. The opportunity for impact is immeasurable when we can relate better to our customers. I look forward to seeing the company continue to employ tenured and new graduate men and women of all colors, nationalities, and cultures, so that unique perspectives can always be shared.*

* * * * *

Post 1

CONGRATULATIONS, FAYE! Wonderful writeup and well-deserving. Wow, very exciting to walk back through your commitment over the many years. Not surprising though to hear about your many successes as I have had the pleasure of being able to work directly with you with The Black Alliance and I have always been astounded by your attention to detail and commitment to everything that we were trying to achieve. Not only could I always count on your support, but I never had to second-guess anything that you agreed to take care of. It is that belief system, drive, and fortitude that I believe has helped to make you successful throughout your career. Continued success to you and yours, Faye. Cheers!

Post 2

Congratulations on thirty years with the company and recognition of your leadership! You are truly a leader within the company and in the community!

Post 3

Congratulations! You are truly an inspiration in so many aspects! You go, girl!

Post 4

Congratulations, Faye. It's an honor to be part of your team. Cheers to many more successful years to come. Great articles. Keep on smiling!

Post 5

We have created some incredible work together, but more importantly had a lot of fun in the process. You have been a great friend and ally, and I am honored to have had the great pleasure to have worked with you.

Post 6

Congratulations, Faye, excellent article. You are an exemplary woman for everyone. It is a pleasure and honor to work with you. I have also learned a lot from you personally, particularly about how to manage people so well that they don't feel managed at all.

Post 7

Congratulations! You've been a big part of my village and a role model which I've always hoped to emulate! Your poise, confidence, intelligence, and wisdom have served as a blueprint for success. I'm proud to have been able to work with you for many years but even more proud that you are my friend.

Post 8

Love it! One of the best leaders I've had the pleasure to work with.

Post 9

She fears God, loves family, a humanitarian, is intentional about her relationships and leads with purpose. Faye, thank you for being a valuable part of my experience. Congratulations on this huge milestone. The company and its customers have benefitted immensely from your humanity and wealth of experience.

Post 10

Thank you for being a fearless leader, a coach and for leading by example. Cheers to many more celebrations, accomplishments, and success stories to come. Cheers to you!

Post 11

Love it! One I really admire her leadership skills. Please accept my deepest thanks for everything you have done and continue to do for us. It is a pleasure to be part of your team.

Post 12

You were one of the reasons I came to work for the company. I was being courted by two other Consulting firms, but my interview with you solidified my choice with the company. The depth of your industry knowledge, the breath of your experience, and the true human qualities that exude when you communicate was charming. I saw my next mentor in you as you did not fit the stereotype of my past leaders in the industry. At the end of our interview, it felt like we had been having a delightful professional conversation that pleasantly ended well.

Coming on your team was a blessing. You are a friend, a leader, a mentor, a fellow child of God, and a big sister. You were always calm and collected even when people deliberately wanted to step on your toes or outtalk you to get a reaction. You carried yourself well in those meetings. You rose above the gender and color. You are respected by many for who you are and the exemplary professional, spiritual, and personal life you lead. You indeed came, saw, and conquered.

Amber, nieces, and young ladies: The building blocks of your reputation should include the fruit of the Spirit, outlined in Galatians 5:22–23: "Love, joy, peace, forbearance, kindness, goodness, faithfulness, gentleness and self-control."

Your reputation will precede you, and it will also be aligned with your legacy. Think of it as a precious jewel that you need to guard and protect. Living with authenticity and integrity should be a guardrail to keep you in check. Let's give them something good to talk about.

This book will end the same way our nights ended. You had to hear your favorite story by Dr. Seuss, *Oh, the Places You'll Go!* I am using his closing line with a personalized twist.

So…
Be your name—Amber, Keisha, Zaniya, or Shay,
You're off to Great Places!
Today is your day!
Your mountain is waiting.
So…get on your way!

PEOPLE WILL TALK

Power scripts

A good name is more desirable than great riches; to be esteemed is better than silver or gold. (Proverbs 22:1)

Commit to the LORD whatever you do, and he will establish your plans. (Proverbs 16:3)

Your beginnings will seem humble, so prosperous will your future be. (Job 8:7)

Personalize your prayer

Lord, help me shape my story so when people talk about me, it will be true and noble.

CHAPTER 14

Reaction from Amber

Around Mother's Day, the number one card or object I would always gravitate toward for my mom would be anything related to Wonder Woman. If she wanted, she could probably start a very mediocre collection of Wonder Woman–themed items. The primary reasons I would do this: (1) Wonder Woman was her favorite superhero. (2) In my youthful eyes, that's all I saw my mother as—a superhero. She was, and still is, confident, fearless, graceful, and beautiful. As I've grown up and grown closer to my mother, and even after reading this book, I feel like comparing her to a superhero is only the shallowest of compliments, and that she is so much more than just a strong figure.

Like an iceberg, we only see a fraction of what people present to us, with so much left hidden from view and yet to be discovered. Growing up, I only saw the glimpse of my mother that a child should see, which was a mother, a caregiver, a friend, and a source of love and protection. Besides the facade of a loving mother, I never really saw what went on outside the doors of our home, such as the discrimination, the injustice, the sexism, the judgment, and the prejudice she faced on a daily occurrence in both the work field and in life as a Black woman in America. She would give life lessons along the way and give small details as to what she faced on a daily basis. However, just like a superhero, she would always shield us from the turmoil of the world and protect us from the evil we would face later in life after growing up. As she mentioned in chapter 1, she, just like many people of color that came before us, was "caught up in the existence of survival with no time to write and offer guidance for others."

This book serves as the part of the iceberg existing underwater that we did not see growing up—the pains of fighting on a daily basis in the corporate world to be viewed as equal to men, when in actuality, she, like so many women, is more qualified than her peers at the work she accomplished. When my mom told me about this book, my first reaction was to cry, primarily because my heart was so full that she would even think about providing advice—both worldly *and* spiritual—to have so that no matter where we are in the world, her words would always be near. It saddens me that she, like many, has gained so much of this wisdom through pain. Yet I am eternally grateful for the lessons that have come from it. This book will forever hold a place in my heart as a tangible piece of love from my mother, and I hope anyone who reads it can also take their pain, frustration, and anger and turn it into something beautiful someday.

To my mom, thank you for being our superhero, our rock, our compass, and our everything. Your grace and elegance through continuous times of storm are beyond admirable, and I am so glad others will see a peak of the resilience that overshadows your superhero facade.

You will always be my Wonder Woman.

ABOUT THE AUTHOR

Faye Irving is an international business consultant helping iconic organizations optimize and transform their operations for greater profitability and empowered customer experiences. During her thirty-five years in corporate America, she has supported over 350 companies. She is a wife and mother of three young adults, but most importantly, she is a child of God looking to always share insight and understanding. Over her business tenure, she has supported more than fifty mentees.